questions

by

Sheri Sherman

Finishing Line Press
Georgetown, Kentucky

questions

Copyright © 2025 by Sheri Sherman
ISBN 979-8-89990-034-1 First Edition
All rights reserved under International and Pan-American Copyright Conventions. No part of this book may be reproduced in any manner whatsoever without written permission from the publisher, except in the case of brief quotations embodied in critical articles and reviews.

ACKNOWLEDGMENTS

Some of the poems in this book have appeared in the following literary journals:

Cutthroat, A Journal of the Arts, "Fall in the garden of Hotel le Pigonnet, Aix-en-Provence, France"

Mudfish, "questions"

The Poetry Miscellany University of Tennessee at Chattanooga, "Saturday morning with Lenny" and "shadows"

My grateful acknowledgments to the editors of these journals and to Finishing Line Press for publishing this manuscript. Also, many thanks to Richard Jackson for his unparalleled mentorship and teaching.

Publisher: Leah Huete de Maines
Editor: Christen Kincaid
Cover Art: Sheri Sherman
Author Photo: Joshua Cohen
Cover Design: Elizabeth Maines McCleavy

Order online: www.finishinglinepress.com
also available on amazon.com

Author inquiries and mail orders:
Finishing Line Press
PO Box 1626
Georgetown, Kentucky 40324
USA

Contents

upbringing	1
the storm	2
strands	3
one afternoon	4
shadows	5
to Van Gogh	6
questions	7
in flux	8
the river	9
water	10
the way	11
bones in the suburbs	12
in a drought	13
insomnia	14
any given week	15
Saturday morning with Lenny	16
Fran	17
the yellow dream	18
the parting	19
clouds	20
questioning time	21
youth remembered from a photo	22
in a canoe at night	23
dreams	25
an orphan in a new land	26
birth of an artist	27
attempted rescue Great Falls, Virginia	28
human trafficking at the border	29
grieving	30
Cora	31
Clyde	32

child's play	33
a haunting at the old big house	34
the farm	35
two crows	36
the feed store	37
the settler's house Saline, Michigan	38
deep down	39
writing	40
fall in the garden of Hotel le Pigonnet Aix-en-Provence, France	41
on Elliot Bay	42
the mustang	43
boundaries	44
waiting	45
thoughts in front of the fireplace	46
the argument	47
for love	48
when the sun shines across the water	49
a love story	50
poem beginning with a pine needle	51
lilacs	52
from the back of my horse at a gallop	53
pops speeding by	54
into night	55
the sugarman	56
peaches	57
dreaming of horses	58
aging	59
the meadow	60
stone wall	61

My enduring thanks to my husband, Steven, and our children, Josh, Hannah, and Kate for their continuous support and encouragement.

upbringing

in the place where I am from   those streets that stain my dreams
caught in shadows   back lit shadows like one of those silhouettes
 illustrations in an old book   where girls were   supposed to learn
how to be a girl   curtsy and pirouette   into the future where it was still ok

to be part of the klan   proud   you scared a little kid to near death
in the fear filled morning   I knew   what it took to beg the growing light
to wait   hold my breath hide   from the seek
and the game to come to an end   in the woods I know
there is a dead cat and the cottonmouth that killed it

the storm

a front is coming in from the sea and the salted wind continues to move through the bougainvillea that looks aside   I wish for cold rain and the sting of wind to come   through the clouds   but worry about the hummingbirds

they must be hiding in the manzanita tree that is currently slapping the hidden sage   that hasn't heard   the storm has found its voice and sings off key   put loud and away   the last remaining slash of blue   a reminder that time has come   to shut the door

feeling the rift   sparrows call from somewhere   I hurry out as the storm overtakes the coast   it needs nothing from me   but what in heaven's name does it mean to love the violent strength that can hurt small birds   even now

I'm done with roofs and doors and beds and so I walk on face to the rain humming

strands

hair from my ponytail released into the breeze   there
I am now part of the universe   that was easy probably
I will be part of a bird's nest or rodent den   fine with me
releasing these words too   after they just blew in   resting   here for a few
these offerings   given and received   hope tangled   in the dna

one afternoon

as soon as it falls from the ledge   the daddy long leg spreads   out all the way down   riding dust particles   for a soft landing   and a new home in the grey vein of the sidewalk   it curls into a ball when the rain starts

from the same crack a dandelion stretches   to drink the distance

                                                                                           between petal and sun

measurable   even with all that gets in the way   and the distance between life   and   death can also be measured   only not until after

shadows grow from the root
    of the day   conflating safety and light

                                                   not easily contained

shadows

I take photos of shadows and steal light from the dusk   of buildings
that lean toward night and an alley   shadows of plants that fall across
sidewalks but not shadows of people   I have no right to their secrets
contrasts stops me every time   but the shades of grey keep me looking
charcoal pewter silver slate ashen   the color absent from a flower
revealing its structure   I once heard someone say that shadows are signs
of aging and that's where   I find the truth

to Van Gogh
after "Cypresses" 1889

when the young grey hawk leaves   it free falls   into a sinking curve to start its flight   off the cliff   then lifts precisely into the tree   I can see now what you saw   when I stare a cypress in a field   the distance makes a difference and I say   to the dying I will ~~heal~~ miss you
    and to the living look   ~~before~~ behind your eyes   lines like rivers flow into a sinuous ~~past~~ future with flotsam of light   catching in little whirlpools before   sinking   or evaporating what do you ~~think~~ see when branches shudder I hope   these hundreds of hues of green stay for a while   how many did you ~~see~~ feel   those vibrations around each ~~leaf~~ needle
    to you sing

questions

what day did your childhood end   what time was it when your dog died   what time did your dad die   your mother your grandmother your great grandmothers   what time was it when you noticed the wind had stopped   when did the wine run out   when was there not a drop of hope to spare   and when did the light drift off   what time was it when

when became

where   the wind changed direction   and the vast field of wheat shifted before my eyes   and so too the eyes followed   and the eyes settled   on a horse on a hill facing into the wind   head bowed mane blowing

how did I come to rest upon this slope with this horse   where the earth is a bed for us both   where answers are stray flakes of snow melting beside me on the thirsty grass   warmed by late life

why hadn't I noticed before

in flux
after Ann Hamilton's "The Event of the Thread," installation/performance art performed at The Park Avenue Armory, New York, NY filmed January 2012.

the air the sounds the curtain a writer and second writer pulleys pigeons in cages swings cables speakers bells a mirror scrolls of paper spilling from the desk a door opening shutting running people people people the audience

                          is

                everything

in the space
        threads crisscross

overandoverandover   again

the curtain is water
the curtain is a cloud
the curtain is air   and in the air

there are bells bells bells

and voices   found

                          and carried in a brown sac

nothing is a cure

            the energizing spirits

                            it may be trivial tomorrow

a series of surprises   *universal moments of*

                            movements of the soul

the river

the leaves of water   oak are tears   falling in waves
to the river   collecting beneath   the log felled
years ago they rush   past the rocks   above the fish and

if fish could cry their tears   would be   tiny pieces of light floating
up to meet the leaves   lifting them   again toward the sky
where they turn   like minnows in currents

today the clouds look   like fish bones   and then leaves

water

after Andy Goldsworthy's sculpture "Icicle Star," Penepont, Dumfriesshires

the cold is one thing to consider   hands freeze in early morning
darkness   fingers swell with saliva   the glue that holds the world
together   it feels like hours   before warmth descends

sustenance   drips through space and stops   captured in a fragile   star
holding everything like the sun   and clouds   and will be soon   gone

the way

not quite lost   in the woods   but getting there and all of a
sudden   aware   of the sun   sliding down the trunks   they look
familiar   the trees with their moss patches   on the north side   I'm
pretty sure   whatever truth is being lost   most of the time involves
darkness

the river to the right still   catches light   like feathers caught in an
updraft   which way

is the wind blowing now   what do I care   and moss doesn't know north
from south   just wants water to drink   branches know of course   they
grow reliably   to the light

it's all about the light   sinking   it's the way   night swims in   leaves
twist   the river grows dark   and I see

I've crossed this path   before   to merge with   the forgotten

and far away

bones in the suburbs

rows of houses like plastic bouquets fan out   stacked waiting for buyers
covering catacombs of years below   here where dogwood trees wave
a hollow greeting   the early sun wears humidity like a wreath hung
around her neck   shards buried centuries ago resurface   bones too   in
a new foundation built upon the old   their enslaved history an acrid
smell   silently rising   from the soil a layer

atop the deep red clay that holds   its own stories   customs   to preserve
tradition and scatter shame   just plaster over   with blessings at the
table   and slip into the future   swimming pools and boxwood hedges
grow in multiples   any chance of

justice has quickly gone   horizontal   half-way across the world
more bones
     planted in ancient ground   dusty by all standards   defeated by
every name   confounded by hope   there   not known for vegetation
but barricades   the Gaza strip

is not a comic   not a funny   not a place in Vegas   but hope   still   a
hope
made by the wind   and rows and rows of young lives   attacked   with
words bullets   bombs
fear rises   vapor   from the hot road   runs backwards   time flung
to the hard ground   gets up covers its head   retreats   and ducks for
cover

in the shrine   sound folds away   she watches mosaics walls weep
shadows and can't   remember when   she last cried   tears   she is
bone dry   bent away   from the sun   already hidden   by smoke in a
grave sky   under   her sandal the dust still moves   above the well of
souls

in a drought

no wonder why I am dying of thirst and can't

get enough when the dam breaks you'll know

how thirsty I was then

I said how I love the rain I told you

it was my memory and I need to remember

the loud whisper of the rapids

the silence of a dark lake

the mist that feeds the wilted wheat

the sound and how it slews through the night

the truth seeps in drop by drop and a dry riverbed waits

insomnia

when I open my mouth anger comes out   so I don't   instead I turn over and try to sleep   I remember when you left the refrigerator door open and walked away   I shut it   doors   slow and silent   or fast slammed   the dark drain of betrayal swirls   thresholds seep away   I walk out of the house into the night and look back   the light from the open door is beautiful clean-edged deep and cold   it spills milk-like onto the tile floor

any given week

Cleveland   Dallas   El Paso   Louisville   Palmdale   Sandy Hook
Minneapolis   Columbus   Tacoma   Atlanta   Rochester   Fort Worth
Ann Arbor   Sacramento   Baton Rouge   Baltimore   Brooklyn
Charlotte   Phoenix

after Friday's shootings   a Saturday morning   fell into Saturday
evening's shootings   that all fell   onto the asphalt   to the sidewalk
into the grass

it isn't until Sunday   that we become aware of the little shards of light
reflecting off the souls   of those lost   and   as we carry flowers to
honor them   we smell the sweet sick
perfume of carnations   that will find us again   in our fitful sleep long
after the sun sets   and on
days when the air is filled with a rising heat

Saturday morning with Lenny

we were listening to the baseball game on the car radio so there's no talking   and I already   knew there's no crying in baseball way before Tom Hanks said so   the loud and running   voices talked strikes and balls and raced the wind from the window   where the metal frame was angry hot so don't touch it stupid its August   and little did we know fifty years later his wife would die the same day   and he would be gone ten years before that   and there was no crying then either   the last time I talked to him   he was yelling curses like fast pitches and flinging rage like curve balls   all strikes   and the hot wind of regret

Fran

she probably died cursing me in her mind since the stroke finally stopped her from saying it all out loud   but there was a lifetime before that filled with her voice   and after death she finds me in my dream where she appears childlike   what else   in a dress she is showing off pointing to the yellow flower on her skirt which is weird because she hated yellow and loved purple   which to this day makes me nauseous   she is standing in the hallway in silence with a smile   the clock next to her once ticked but now just hums in a nonstop high pitch faint and pink

the yellow dream

we met and went to a white house that smelled of citrus perfume   I didn't recognize my own home   and yet I knew my way around and that was the scent I wore   we entered a bedroom maybe a parlor where   I laid a black suitcase on the bed maybe a table   and opened it up   inside was a folded silk taffeta maybe organza   dress of a bright marigold yellow   singing I picked it up   from blooms of canary yellow daffodils and held it up to the light   maybe I should have put it on   and was it raining out   or was that snow   turning yellow from the sun that slanted both inside and out   inside where the lemon chiffon air filled the room and beyond the windowpane   metallic gold particles froze

the parting

a wandering star   rose in the east   and the silent wind   streamed backward   into the mist that parted against its will   when I walked the streets   the dark pressing one cheek   the purple street slowly dilating toward the trees that stretched for bits of light   houses reluctant to wake

lit windows that smoldered   within me for hours—

all through the day   I was hungry for stories hiding   behind frost and dirt mouths searching for brewed coffee   burnt toast   cold meat from the night before—

that night at dinner I ate too much and laughed so hard—
as if the past didn't happen

clouds

the eye of the dragon is a long slit that becomes a river whose current is swift its waves roll fast   the riverbed shies   away in fear   silt roils underneath its length   and the clouds exhale   fire

entering the hospital   that would be the last she sees of   the sky

questioning time

how much time does there need to be   to move from seeing   to feeling to knowing   is it the heart that makes the leap   or the mind   that lives in   explores   that space between   where moments stack up   angry little waves   pushing   each other into   not quite silence   a sloosh of energy   from one to the next   the wavelength measured   impatience does not serve   save for the sake of momentum   the bird's shadow flies on the water   is it the bird   or time passing   it swims the trough and is gone

into   this moment

youth remembered from a photo

and when night came and everyone left   the universe fractured   and we maybe sensed   it would never be the same   starts piled up like years   and pods fell from the tree in   desperation to continue   but there it was   drifting   over everyone's head   floating out over the meadow   to the old chestnut tree   stretched wide   over the dirt path   over empty rows and rows   from the trophy ceremony   among the daises and clover   they all heard laughter   and felt our desire   and mistook it for the afternoon's humidity

there are more   snapshots continue   to fade to prove   the day was real once

in a canoe on a lake at night

my hands play on the surface

                                        in moon-mottled foam

                                                                                     paddles resting in the hull

lying off the shore

                            sight doubts but wind confirms

                                                             location as if it matters

I turn to look

                  back the edge looms a thin black line

                                            the dark

helps me find my place my eyes

                              roam the stars and the waves

                                                      lull as the wind

reads

between the lines I float

                          point to the sky name

                                        stars like cousins we talk

about the rocks the soil sediment

                              dust the fate of earth and this drop of water

          someone asks who cares

and confer

    its late and everyone is fading so slowly

            I close my eyes

and dip my fingers into

     the deep water beneath me

dreams

after "A Girl Asleep" by Johannes Vermeer, 1657

don't let the smooth surface fool you   she is full of dreams
tempting   as the fruits just beyond her fingertips
her chest barely moves   she's hiding within herself   from what
it's her secret   dreams slipped under the tablecloth   heavy with so many
days full of tedious work   that crimson suggests anger
brushed and delicate anger   caressed   by darkening air
but look   her fichu flutters about her neck
from some unseen window   flung open   the hot summer evening breeze
finds its edge and   nudges her into a liminal hope

she's floating under a peach sky   on the surface of a plum lake
the trees make such a perfect shade   she wakes to thirst

an orphan in a new land

why in such a flat land does the river wind   so recklessly
and crumbs swept off the ledge with care still fall   so savagely
I toss them in the water   watch the hungry rapids eat
each and every one   only then can I see   how loss becomes
silence

I knew the current   would never let me cross   food and water would
never taste the same   and this coarse orphan's blanket   how can it
mean both warmth and rejection

birth of an artist
after the painting, Morganthau Plan, 2012 by Anselm Keifer

there in the cellar beneath   the house surrounded   by deep wood and rubble   I am born   knowing   the sight of blood   on the snow that wets the fields   I feel the shafts of dried wheat   in the paint my hands slippery   pressing down mixed   ash the light   oozing forth grazing the tips   colors begin to bloom on the canvas   I am mixed to a muddy color March 8 1945

I hear a voice say *it's always construction demolition then construction* and realize I am talking years into the future   guilt is acidic and I am caught between the light and the dark   black forest of Germany it shines with the smell of death yet   I accept life

yellow hurts my eyes   these stems too bright for this world

attempted rescue Great Falls, Virginia

when the river finally gave up   its dead returned to us

we were freezing   wet up to our chins   and the fish were mad
at the intrusion   like the mist   they didn't care   if another person
drowned

and the falls didn't care   the rush of water hissed   *more will die*

we walked away and cried alone
the fish have learned to ignore the ghosts climbing over the rocks

human trafficking at the border

orchids from the florist grow into tight pots   look   the blooms open white touched with yellow   caged in hot breath they stand   defiant roots push   inside ceramic   and lean to their future   of cracks and compost

but for a moment   demand the struggle   for survival

grieving

    I knew lies when I heard them   Snow White was raped in her sleep and never woke up   Cinderella had feet like none I ever saw and didn't make it back ~~home~~   I hated fairytales   and candy   I loved the dark   ink   and everything Sir Arthur wrote   that's what I called him when I was eight   I refused to read anything else   except for Dante   my hurt hurt everyone else too much   when I ~~went away~~ was orphaned they tried   to feed me happy endings   but when Watson said Holmes had a horror of destroying documents I knew   I could trust him   to find ~~the truth~~   meaning   in the dark   the scent of an old book   and Dante   being familiar with heaven and hell   knew not to lie to me

Cora

once I saw her glance over her shoulder at me   a little white girl   she
a big black lady laughing   because I told her I wanted to be just like her
fierce   and patient like a cherry tree   she loved cherries   washed
and dripping with cold water   soft pink flesh that sweetens only on the
branch   she knew patience   I see her shoulders move back and her
glare fixed upon some white face telling her   what to do   frowning she
gets real close and   shoves a pit into his open mouth and waits for the
cough

Clyde

he was so tall   when I looked at him I had to throw my head back   so far I'd see the sun in place of his face   he took care of the yard and I following his long legs   helped pull weeds and   laughed when he laughed

but the neighbors didn't see what was so funny how can he be trusted with a little white girl where was her mother   no matter this went on for years despite all the stares   whispers   threats   then he was gone one morning

and I have worried about him from that day   on a never ending was he ok each day   the sun is high and strong I think of him

child's play

I spent my entire childhood   wishing   I was a wild animal
a jaguar   solitary   I would have a bite fit to take a caiman down   my
teeth would puncture straight through a skull   or a cheetah   the fastest
from a crouch   a 100 mph in five seconds kind of torrent   I could outrun
anything
                                   my black tears useful in the open

or wolf   senses always   on alert   singing   at night no one could sneak
up from behind   capable of true love   or a fox smart quick light on its feet
I could escape under the moon   or a hare with ears large enough to hear a
breath or a step
or a porcupine   needles that walk   to repel the slightest touch
                            I could sleep then

but oh to take flight   to be a bee with wings small and swift   to spend the
day kissing flowers
or a hawk   to see life from a long way up   there at last   I'd ride the wind far
and away
                                        high into the light

no one knew   in my head I would wander the world   the steep mountains
and deep forests plains and fields   the distant sky   fearless in snow and
rain and heat and storms   where I was

                            free

a haunting at the old big house

I'd use the back door but I don't want to scare anyone　　and spirits don't
actually walk through walls　　especially ones beneath haint blue porches
something about that color　　it's confusing as to what's ceiling and water
or sky so just open the back door now

the kitchen is ginger warm though I don't feel　　the cold here in the yard
just weary　　but you know　　the walls will continue to speak
with delicate laughter and clinking plates　　stemmed glasses
softy mingling　　and white gloved hands folded

the children still whistle while they walk　　the hot soup in blue China
bowls from the kitchen　　oh the anticipation of pudding
aflame with brandy　　but gone so quickly like the smell of smoke
and the steam from the boiling tea poured—

fine I'll just step into the twilight　　softly so as not to leave a trace
of fear on the snow where your prints lead　　to the door but time will fill
them just like mine it will be no longer　　what it was
faint flecks of ice and light　　stretched low along the horizon

there you'll drift out of sight as the shapes fade behind you
feel the cosmic dust on your face　　and touch the edge of a cloud

the farm

the old sod farm was built long ago before the place had a name
made from the forest that used to stand where the corn does now
in their haste did the settlers know

the names of the trees they used   beech basswood poplar oak to keep
themselves safe from the wild country they said   god must have loved
those Indians blamed for everything that went wrong   why be afraid of
god's kind children the kids loved looking for arrowheads in the field

we bought the house from a lady who wore blue tip to toe
and baked blueberry muffins every Sunday   she lived and loved on plush
blue carpet and saw   them at the edge of the field before each storm
returning to the lost forest

the wind flew angry across the land   made a clear path
into the house   I knew the ghosts would come   for shelter or
conversation to heal those old wounds   I show them out when the sky
turns blue

two crows

1
mean good news   I've been told   I see them flying   west across a dull sky
   west the little death of the day   an ending one crow is found dead   this is
not comforting

the other crow is picking at the clouds like crumbs

2
two crows flew west   across a dull sky   one crow was found
dead in a neighbor's pool   an eye fixed on the sinking sun   half concealed
by clouds
matted with rain

at night the sea   a disembodied voice   relentless   wave after wave   *it's no
use give up*
sets of three keep time   this is not comforting
stars hide in the gloaming for solace   a home   however brief   however
dank

dripping   the stars slip into my eyes

the feed store

watch the animals because they're filled with grace
the old farmer said and looked straight at me
can a feed store be a sacred place

where they don't go you don't go—to that space
they won't graze—those mounds beyond the cedar tree
watch the animals because they're filled with grace

it wasn't right how they were displaced
aren't we all afraid of not being free
can a feed store be a sacred place

the horses hate to be in their stall no trace
of sweet grass only wind that smells of history
watch the animals because they're filled with grace

in the cold morning the horses come face to face
with gloved hands that feed them timothy
can a feed store be a sacred place

I'm off again to that holy place
like my horse's eyes it helps me see
watch the animals because they're filled with grace
can't a feed store be a sacred place

the settler's house Saline, Michigan

through doors and doors they all moved and followed   the need for shelter   corners and lines planks laid   boards beams   seams of life wooden floors and plaster walls   clay bricks set atop a stone basement earth house   layers and layers   of sweat and despair   dried solid years and years ago   when they went to plow the vast west

                                                the woods wild and watching every move

deep down

I want to think spring days   will keep coming back in endless rows   of years
and years   like the maze I stand in   reaching   way past my shoulders
rows of rows of planted seasons   predictable   despite the combine and
thresher slashing and beating summer   I know deep down   a seed
or two will hide and grow   the fallow field will green

here I am standing on the edge of the field   feeling the warmth
of the winter sun for the seed

writing

in the middle of the day   I start to sweep the middle of the room   drift
outward to the edge   muddled and move dust on to the next room
and the next until   I'm on the porch bent   around the house

all else becomes the center

when I drop the broom   bits of straw blow off the ledge   and lift
into the sky   like contrails traversing the daytime moon   beyond the rail
a scent grows up while roots reach   the centrifugal search
for water droplets deep   within the earth   wild lilies spread fast
drinking searching looking   back to the cirrus clouds

fall in the garden of Hotel Le Pigonnet, Aix-en-Provence, France

two white turtle doves in a black iron cage in the middle

of the garden thick with the smell of fall rain and old moss

one listless in the dusk deep in retreat her dark eyes drift

up as the shadows of late days and tall cypress lean down

dawn is dimmed sinking into rain and a dove

gone dead I imagine how

heavy it feels to fall to lie on the cold floor then light

in hand trees turn away and the wind moves on

nothing more but the cries short and a pause then slow

and long her mate's wings lifted by the slight

stir the yellow leaves of the ginkgo tree against the musky sky turn

and I wake to fluttering in my chest and the sound of wings on metal

on Elliot Bay

the boat falters   against the wind   its strength is beyond   direction the far shore a landscape varnished with fog and a future   the waves the shore the ghosts billions of years of water sand and rock become   this moment when time is   tarnished and dense   sands shift rocks yield

to water   wave after wave   they push the day into the dark   and wind the wind has time by the throat

birthed in the dark it drags along   whatever it can   rising sinking spinning from the hidden sun

the mustang

my 1976 silver blue glow mustang slid on the slush   and banked into
the snow piled up the night before   the whir of police lights   flung
onto a searing sky spun minutes into a thicket of years

and years later in Virginia I saw a shadow fly over   the cut hay fields a
hawk and an old love   asked me about that old mustang   sweeping the
dirt road with my foot I thought

of our last kiss under the hawthorn tree   its sanguine haws brushing
the veined trunk   and the thorns hiding beneath the now
fire-bright leaves burning into the still white clouds

boundaries

how do we know   the earth a field a body   before we crumble dirt in our hands and scar the ground with a stick   do we know   where the edge of the leaf punctures air   where particles hit and part

we see fog pushes in   to caress the sun   this is how we know   what we know of love   all touch is friction   and a cut

waiting

Hannah the child sitting in a field   picking tiny flowers gently
slowly from within the grass white blooms   floating on the pond
of her shiny palm   pink with happiness she holds
the day giving all   her attention to those wet petals   unaware of the
sky stretched above   and beyond a future full   of the nourishment of
sunlight

how do I know this?   I am her mother and can see

the bright cerulean blue surrounding   her as it fades into a smudge
of marigold at the horizon where   a murder of crows grazes the cirrus
clouds and they hold the curdling wind   under their wings paint the air
dark as a swarm of bees no bird would touch   instead they fade into
the buzzing storm   I hold back at the end of my arm

thoughts in front of the fireplace

the flames melt the snow   still clinging between the grain

while I turn in your arms   safe before the window

look how the flakes cut   into the snow's fresh flesh

it isn't the snow   falling silent

or the falling of your breath   or the flutter of hair

on your arm against my cheek   that makes me think of white sheets

wrinkling beneath our weight   it's not the blue

shadows falling like tears   beneath the eyes of the world

and slipping between its trees   but the melting tracks

of thought dripping through   the glow of your forehead

the argument

1. breakfast   peering across the kitchen table   I handed you a second cup of coffee   after all I
can be sweet sometimes   still why not have some bitter dialogue   a scene remembered
    from last night's disagreement   to compliment your seedless jam   oh you thought we had a
good talk   just look at my face   as I fold this napkin and place it on my plate

I stared outside for so long   I watched the sky brighten
streaks deepening deepening   I didn't even notice you left

2. lunch   I lied   I knew you were gone and   I savored the silence
that followed me into the afternoon   cold as the bologna on white left in the frig   two days   a light wind came through the door   we pretended it all smoothed itself over   until the third night

3. in the pitch dark we talked   with long silences   I counted stars from bed   the window frame made everything seem finite   the sky would clear that up

many days into the future   will we know   what gets solved   in the meantime I offer you a plate of clouds

for love

don't get me diamonds   don't buy a necklace
I don't need earrings to   live or love   find me instead a meadow full
of wet air and a fawn   so I can live like that   place full of sunlight and
moon and many shades of dark

would you rub me   against the honeysuckle vine   and feed me
new soft pieces   of grass sweet to start each new   day with a bud green
breeze blowing past my fear   taken downwind away   from those who
wish me harm

when the sun shines across the water

just as this westerly breeze embraces my face surely you would
and as the fading sun holds me still you would
and as the deepening tide wraps my hips I know your hands would
seeing the light has always made a path across the bay
to offer the scent of night and salt to our hair and lips

a love story

the bent grass meant spring and we   lazy lawned hips pressed down
looking up into the sun blind   melted wings were raw spent
spinning on the wind   when fall leaves fell like love
and carelessly cracked   blinded by the winter harmed
our youth yellowed   from the roots   time snuck between our lips

this time this taste   like hindsight now   I gather in my arms the leaves
the grass the wind the light   the many springs ours   again are
greening

poem beginning with a pine needle

Merwin says where I'm going

                    is farther at every step so when I rest

                                      my head against

the sky

words blow in and slap my face

                    with soft hands I wonder

                                  where have they been

heard

before over the fields or

          through the boughs around

                            the stars and where birds

parley

and parry there in the tree

          top branches of full pines

                                          tap the

clouds then light

      begins to bend into

          my open ear and I hear a needle fall

                              at my feet

lilacs

it smells like my mother's lilacs   in a closed room with no vase
the woods in spring were lush   with lilacs   and an impatient creek
let the reek of rotting wood lay   hushed beside the ~~fallen~~ felled tree
this is where the stale air is exhaled

and suddenly makes sense   like a sigh after all   isn't it the breath
that makes the life   or is it life that makes the breath   I only ~~know~~
remember   the scent rising

when she died they found   a tiny violet flower on her eye

from the back of my horse at a gallop
for Jackie

the eye runs across the wet grass and the center lengthens   beneath a blur fast-forward
    bolt   painting a rain of hooves   light and quick as the hands and a thought   this whir of green and blue earth   flows   the beginning a brush the end a stroke   and the middle
    flecks of dirt and dew   fly   with the mane   reins mouths   open the sky   splashes wind

                      sound   floats
away

trees clouds collide and merge   a field of crystals grow mid-air   with the sting of cold and the gleam of sun   the distance blues   and the past greens fast and falls back   a blaze

a touch on the flanks slight as a fly   and the leap   legs and girth and rider become

space and air and light

Pops speeding by

the speed through which he traveled his life was as fast as his midget racer would carry him   I'll never know that exact number of miles per hour   but I do know it was just as fast off that dirt oval as on it and   so it goes around and around   I have always moved as fast as I could and was never afraid of the dirt or the dark or death because that's where he is   I think of this when I see a comet flying between the stars just points to mark the speed

into night
after Eugene O'Neill, Long Day's Journey into Night

"the fog is where I wanted to be..."

condensation on the glass grows   throughout the night   drips of water
cut a line   of sight filled   with pearl leeward lights   spindrift off the
dark waves beyond   the window seals with fog   off the sea a ghost
within a ghost   within the self   the room a stage darkened

who wants to see life as it is...   it feels good to be lost in the fog that heals
it anesthetizes the gibbous mind   despite the need for loss
and being lost   something   slips and opens out   to the soundless
night

the sugarman
after the song "Sugarman" by Sixto Rodriguez

he's not hungry   but rain sounds   like rice krispies sinking
into milk   sugar on the bottom   his belly is the heavy part of a
water drop it splits on the edge of a spoon   and slips   into the dark
grounded night he dips his foot into a puddle   at the bottom of the
street   dull white light dusts the asphalt   no need to look up he knows
all the answers and sees the coin   glimmer silver under the cold surface
and opens the diner door

peaches

they are all about summer   the sweet distant smell clinging   to
memory and the golden sphere mocks the mid-day sun   for not having
any taste she always had me stand   over the sink to eat it   what way
is that to enjoy a peach   no   I needed to be under the heat of the
afternoon glaring from the tops of dandelion leaves   the juice dripping
to the sidewalk where I could share it with the bees

she was allergic to bees and was afraid   of anything that could leave a
mark on her delicate skin   the flesh of expensive fruit   she frowned
at my tan wet arms   and the red streak in every sunset
and on the side of my peach   but she took a tiny bite after all and smiled
for a split second   watching   the flesh start to tear   beneath my teeth

dreaming of horses

on the side of the river   and on the banks   there are wisps of grass
and the water moves   along with the sound of stems breaking
the horses   scattered about   they tear at sweet shoots always famished
and trot head up

to smell predators near   or far   and further they wander
into the field   and sky   the day a trough deep and not ever empty

she plucks my heart like it's an apple picked off the tree an ear flicks the
fly away nostrils search the ground   her flanks tense   the mare starts
and bolts through my chest and over the hill

aging

here I am with my scars   and scrapes my self   inflicted age of grey
and brittle love   left treading in a rip tide of oceanic dreams
this rends me   so spent   after emerging from my bent and cresting
sleep I live   until I am young   so young it feels like   pins and needles
because my heart was asleep

the meadow

in the woods I follow the creek around the rocks   slick with spring   at the edge of the meadow new leaves and shade   a line as strong as a promise   and as sweet   the day like young grass held between the teeth a blade of sun on my lips

the fawn moves from beneath   across the grass shadow to light stunned and slightly bristled she stops   turns   an ear twists   the rocks wait

I hear the water spill the afternoon over the trees   the sky sees   the young and the swift and the lea a hollow the wind fills   she's gone

the light fades   as I watch   over the rocks and the shade and the meadow

stone wall

a turn of words   an upturning   there in the forest of sleep   become stones that become   a stone fence at the edge of the wood   climbing the ridge and then   disappearing

into the earth   diving into its subterranean space   as it becomes a sinuous being with mica scales   the stone layer's logic becomes fluid down there where words become song

long drawn-out notes that resurface   through the soil some unseen breathing hole   found by feeling   a resurrection into air   a still and cloudless sky

waking to land it meanders along   a steady gait   but growing in strength a growing thing   a moving stream   and the echo of rock   stacked and stacked and stacked
fit by what hand   all along the minutes of a dream   and later in the pasture light

the wall becomes a poem that walks the horizon

Acknowledgments

Some of the poems in this book have appeared in the following literary journals:

Cutthroat, A Journal of the Arts, "Fall in the garden of Hotel le Pigonnet, Aix-en-Provence, France"

Mudfish, "questions"

The Poetry Miscellany University of Tennessee at Chattanooga, "Saturday morning with Lenny" and "shadows"

My grateful acknowledgments to the editors of these journals and to Finishing Line Press for publishing this manuscript. Also, many thanks to Richard Jackson for his unparalleled mentorship and teaching.

An MFA writing graduate of Vermont College of Fine Arts, **Sheri** has worked as a copywriter and freelance journalist. Having lived in every region of the United States, she grew up in Virginia and now resides in San Diego and Vermont. Sheri graduated with a B.A. in English Literature from American University in Washington D.C. Prior to beginning her MFA, she attended the summer Iowa Writer's Workshop. Her poetry has been published in *Cutthroat, A Journal of the Arts* and *Poetry Miscellany,* U-T Chattanooga. A critical essay was published in *The Asheville Poetry Review* as well as a literary paper in the Ljubljana University Journal in Slovenia. Her micro fiction piece, "Hospital Stay," was published in *On the Run*. Sheri's landscape photography and poetry feature the natural world and her interest in how time and space are experienced within our landscapes, our senses, and the human consciousness.

www.ingramcontent.com/pod-product-compliance
Lightning Source LLC
Chambersburg PA
CBHW030058170426
43197CB00010B/1577